How to Draw
People

Barbara Soloff Levy

DOVER PUBLICATIONS, INC.
Mineola, New York

Note

It's fun to draw pictures of animals, flowers, and cars, but what about drawing people? It's not as hard as you think! Each page in this book shows you how to build a picture of a person from simple shapes. For example, page 2 begins with a head and an arm. Once you have drawn these, you add fingers and a foot. Then you draw another foot. Finally, you add some lines for a face and more fingers, as well as buttons for the clothing. Now you have a drawing of a baby!

You may want to trace the steps of each picture first, just to get a feel for drawing. There is a helpful Practice Page facing each drawing page. Then you can begin to make your drawing using a pencil with an eraser. Keep adding shapes until you get to the end, and your drawing is finished. Then erase the dotted lines. When you are pleased with your drawing, you can go over the lines with a felt-tip pen or colored pencil. After you complete your drawings, you can enjoy them even more by coloring them in.

When you feel comfortable drawing, look around you and try to draw pictures of some of the people you see. Ask your family and friends to pose for you. Remember to look for the simple shapes that make up the body. Then add some details to make the drawing look real. Keep on drawing, and have fun!

Bibliographical Note

How to Draw People is a slightly altered republication of the edition published by Dover Publications, Inc., in 2002. "Practice Pages" have been added for this edition.

International Standard Book Number

ISBN-13: 978-0-486-42060-8
ISBN-10: 0-486-42060-4

Manufactured in the United States by Courier Corporation
42060413   2014
www.doverpublications.com

How to Draw
People

2　Baby boy

Practice Page

4   Baby girl

Practice Page

6 Boy

Practice Page

8   Girl with doll

Practice Page

Practice Page

12 Baseball player

Practice Page

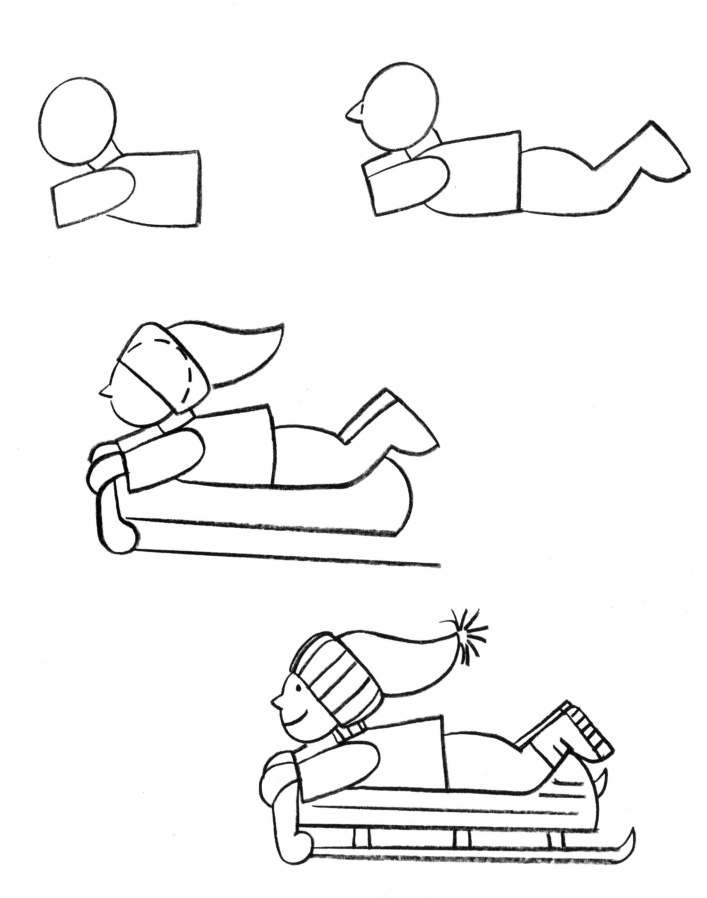

14   Child on sled

Practice Page

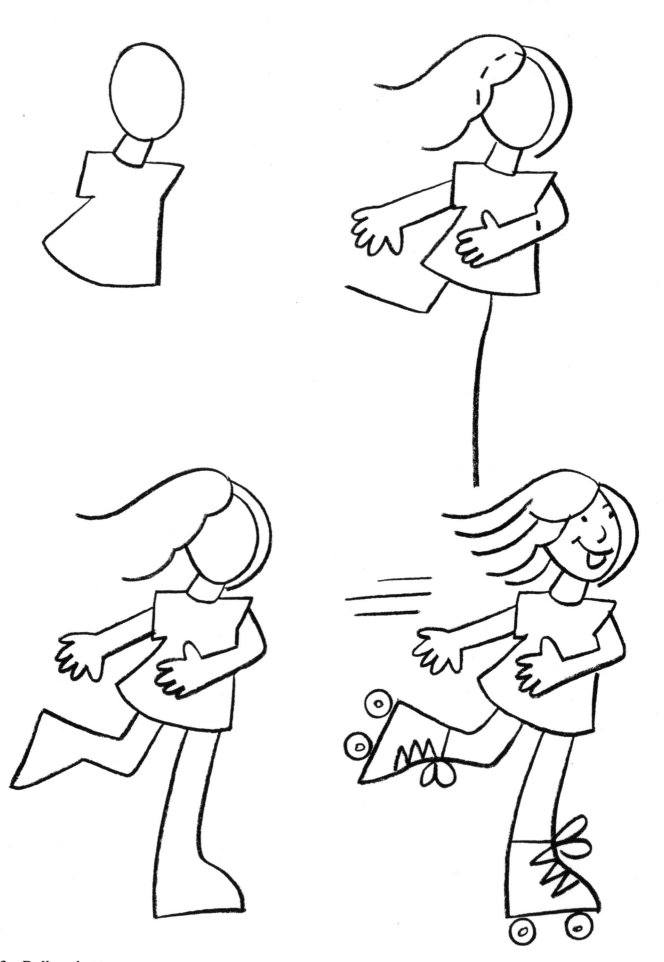

Practice Page

18 Boy on swing

Practice Page

20   Girl with fishing rod

Practice Page

22   Boy with toy train

Practice Page

24   Child with kite

Practice Page

Practice Page

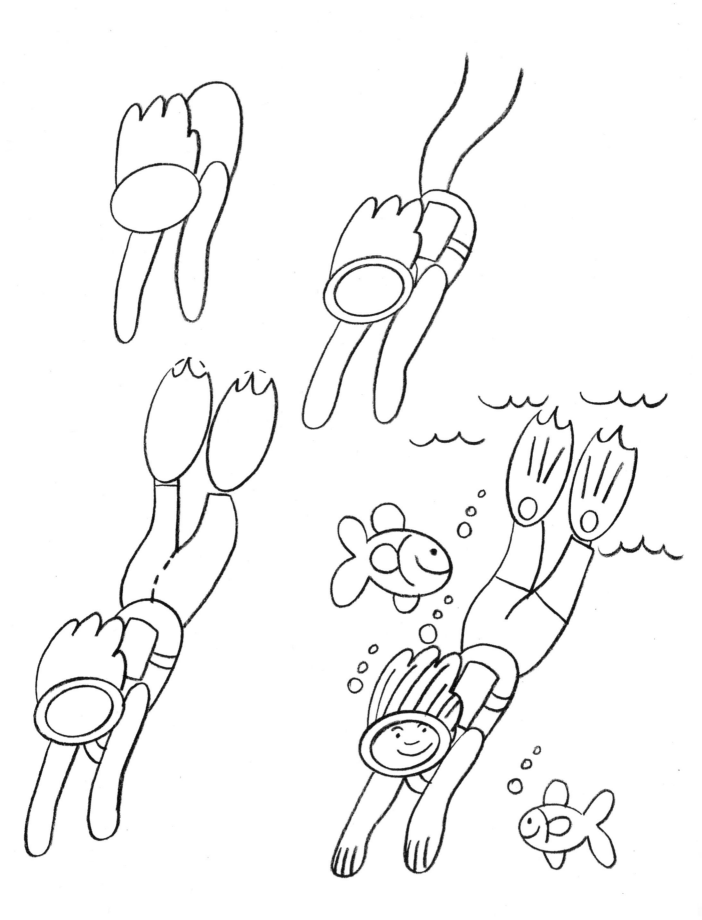

Practice Page

30   Tennis player

Practice Page

32   Skateboarder

Practice Page

Practice Page

36 Boy with beach ball

Practice Page

38   Marching band drummer

Practice Page

40 Hiker

Practice Page

Practice Page

44   Postal worker

Practice Page

46   Ice cream man

Practice Page

48   Woman with cake

Practice Page

Practice Page

Practice Page

Practice Page

Practice Page

58 Dancer

Practice Page

Practice Page